St. Helens Libraries

Please return / renew this item by the last date shown.
Books may also be renewed by phone and Internet.

Telephone – (01744) 676954 or 677822
Email – centrallibrary@sthelens.gov.uk
Online – http://eps.sthelens.gov.uk/rooms

This Is Ephemera

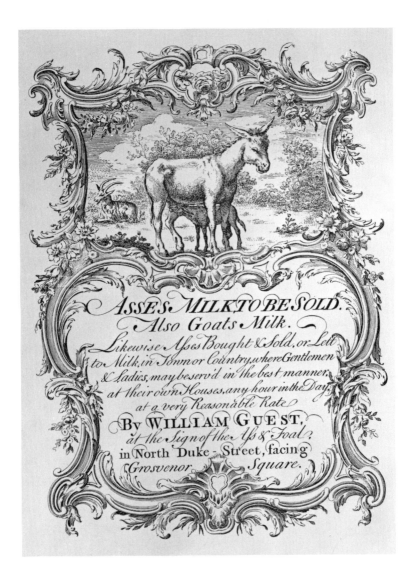

This Is Ephemera

Collecting Printed Throwaways

Maurice Rickards

David & Charles
Newton Abbot   London

The ephemera illustrations in this book are from the collections of
Stephen and Janet Greene, Calvin Otto, Frank Teagle, and the author.

British Library Cataloguing in Publication Data
Rickards, Maurice
  This is ephemera
  1. Printed ephemera—Collectors and collecting
  I. Title
  769'.5   NC1280
  ISBN 0–7153–7672–1

First published in the USA by The Stephen Greene Press,
Brattleboro, Vermont

First published in the UK by David & Charles, 1978

This edition is published by special arrangement with
The Stephen Greene Press, Brattleboro, Vermont

Printed in Great Britain by
Redwood Burn Limited Trowbridge & Esher
for David & Charles (Publishers) Limited
Brunel House Newton Abbot Devon

Contents

TRADE CARD, C. 1880

Foreword

First, the word itself—*ephemera*. It comes, to us through Latin from the Greek *epi* (about), and *hemeris* (day). The word presents three major problems. In the first place there is some uncertainty as to how to say it. In the second, there is uncertainty among many people as to what it means. In the third, there is uncertainty as to whether it is singular or plural. With qualifications like these, the word seems an unlikely candidate for popular usage. But the fact is that more and more people are using it, and we might as well face it.

Broadly speaking, the word, *ephemera*, is used to denote the transient everyday items of paper—mostly printed—that are manufactured specifically to use and throw away. Tickets—bus, train or theater tickets—are a typical form of ephemera, vital when they are needed, wastepaper immediately afterwards. They flourish for a moment and are done. As with the mayfly (the *ephemerid*), which lives but for a day, theirs is a brief and modest glory.

So much for meaning—though, as we shall see, the word is applied to a vast range of items, some of them more ephemeral than others. As to pronunciation, there are two contending versions: some favor "e*femm*era," others "e*feem*era." On the whole, *"femm"* seems the first to be winning out. The Ephemera Society (who should, presumably, know) say "e*femm*era," though they also magnanimously admit "e*feem*era".

As to the singular and plural status of the word *ephemera,* the position is a little ragged. Strictly the word is the plural of *ephemeron* (one *ephemeron;* two *ephemera*) but ephemeron survives today only in the most strictly limited academic application. In popular parlance *ephemera* alone has survived. We therefore find ourselves using such roundabout forms as "an item of ephemera," and such inaccurate ones as the title of this book. (More grammatically acceptable would be *These* Are *Ephemera.* But for the plain-speaking ephemerist, *This Is Ephemera* sounds more sensible.)

As for the word "ephemerist," used to denote the student and collector of ephemera—and used, incidentally, as the title of the ephemera-collectors' journal—here, too, there is a snag. To be exact, an ephemerist was in former times concerned with the daily positions of celestial bodies. (Again we see the presence of "the day" as a basic element.) An "ephemeris" was an almanac in which the heavens' moods and motions were outlined. The contemporary use of "ephemerist" to describe a paper-oddments-specialist is a novelty. But as with all such novelties, we may expect that usage will shortly hallow it. The word has clearly come to stay.

TRADE CARD, C. 1830

1

The World of Printed Oddments

The ephemera of everyday life includes, as we have seen, much more than tickets. In pursuit of its daily affairs, society produces a vast range of printed miscellany. Hardly a transaction or encounter takes place without the by-product of a piece of printed paper. Bills, receipts, statements, delivery notes, compliment slips, price lists, memos, advertising material—mankind generates each day a paper snowstorm.

This everyday material has much more than passing validity. Above and beyond its immediate purpose, it expresses a fragment of social history, a reflection of the spirit of its time. As with all other human records, as with the fashion-plate itself, its style is soon out of date. In a decade or two—sometimes in only a year or two—we may return to it with incredulity: Was that really the way things were? So much change in so short a time? These fragments, rescued, conserved, and displayed by the collector, may form a graphic social record—an encapsulated visual history.

The full range of ephemera-collector's items is vast. It includes such widely varying items as labels, printed notices, trade cards, laundry lists, certificates, summonses, bills of lading, licenses, indentures, permits, rent demands, timetables, tax forms, wrappers and packaging, advertising material, menus, notices to quit, mobilization papers, membership cards, death warrants, school reports, mourning cards, greeting cards, magazines and newspapers, posters, stickers, stationery, parking tickets, touring maps, scraps—the full spectrum of life expressed in miscellany.

For the most part these are inexpensive items—fragments salvaged from attic or wastebasket—or, in the case of today's ephemera, acquired free of charge in the daily round. Advertising and promotion contribute much ephemera. So do bureaucracy and Law and Order. So do various forms of transportation, the entertainment industry, and sport and spectacle. To a flux of apparently trivial scraps of paper the collector brings his own contribution—order, and a sense of history.

In even greater need of the collector's touch are the rarer, older items of ephemera. These, the "specials" of ephemera collecting, are the early 19th-Century slave delivery notes, the anti-cholera recipes and the pauper's bread-line tickets. As well as order, collecting these needs money too—or a great deal of browser's luck. Their rarity and significance make them hard to find in wastebaskets and costly to buy from those who got there first.

But not all early ephemera is scarce and expensive. We do well to remember that even in earlier times most items were printed in quantity—certainly in hundreds, often in thousands—and very few items have not their kith and kin lurking somewhere else.

Nineteenth-century tax forms, for example, with their evocative listings of taxes on windows and hair powder, are by no means uncommon. Nor are quack-medicine labels, or tax forms demanding payment for the provision of street night watchmen. Apprentices' indentures, too, with their strictures on gaming and fornication, are still to be found fairly easily.

The appeal of ephemera is not necessarily in its extreme rarity or great age. It is rather in the mind and eye of the collector, for whom it serves as a spark to the imagination. An 18th-Century blacksmith's receipt has no formal market value. It is a human document that speaks, or does not speak, depending on who you are.

Ephemera may be said to fall into three main groups: the truly transient (the ticket, the price tag, the coupon); the semi-durable (the playing card, the share certificate, the calendar), and the keep-it-forever (the mourning card, the commemorative souvenir).

As a general rule, these groups show design-awareness in inverse ratio to their transience. The ticket, here today and gone tomorrow, is a job printer's do-it-yourself concoction. The calendar, with claims to a life of at least a month or two, may have pretensions to attractiveness. The keep-it-forever commemorative may even aspire to "art." (We may note in passing that there are some collectors who would not admit commemorative material as ephemera; others would also reject the semi-durables. But that, for the moment, is another matter.)

Admitted or not, we see in these categories an ascending order of self-consciousness. We also see that many of the most engaging items of ephemera are those that state their purpose without guile. For the collector of "primitives" there is no reality quite so real as the 1830's turnpike ticket or the blacksmith's business card—misprints, thumb-prints and all.

And yet can anyone ignore the elegance, the outrageous magnificence, of the 18th- and 19th-Century billhead? These works of art, custom-engraved for any Tom, Dick or shopkeeper, are luxuries far beyond the call of business duty. To call them ephemera is to do them small justice, yet there is no doubt that they were viewed in their time as throwaways. The law of the inverse ratio of permanence to artistry is not watertight. Even the humble admission ticket (some of them designed by artists of distinction) may qualify as a work of art.

CENTENNIAL EXHIBITION TICKET, 1876

There can be no final opinion as to what constitutes ephemera and what does not. If transience is the only touchstone, what of children's board-games, bookplates, passports—all of them collector's items, none of them more than slightly transient? And what of cigarette cards and other such serial items, designed not merely to keep, but specifically to *collect*? And postcards, originally produced for utility, later also to collect? And postage stamps?

Broadly speaking, cigarette cards, match covers, postcards, and postage stamps are viewed as self-contained worlds of their own. With their own journals, their own well established societies and study groups, they form major specialist fields in themselves,

MOURNING CARD, 1883

each embracing further sub-specializations. We also see that in each of these categories there has been a more or less clear-cut history of casual utility developing into self-conscious "collectibility."

Cigarette cards, at first produced in random bursts but soon in numbered sets, epitomise the trend. Postcards, too, at first a communications medium, were soon to generate the postcard-album industry. Much the same has happened to postage stamps where, in recent times, the collectors market has added a major source of revenue to the world's post offices. These categories must indeed be admitted as ephemera—but ephemera of a special order of self-consciousness.

In any attempt to define what is and what is not ephemera it must sooner or later be conceded that there are gray areas in which opinions must differ. One thing only may be said with any certainty: on the whole the ephemerist tends to stick to two dimensions rather than three. Uniform buttons and other heavyweight durables are out. (Though we may note that, perversely, jeans labels, election buttons and packaging are in.)

Packaging is the most obvious exception to the two-dimension rule. Here, by common consent, ephemerality outweighs all else; pack and package, label and showcard—virtually the whole in-store phenomenon—come under the ephemerist's eye. Here, as much as anywhere, the passing trends of the social scene are reflected. Here, too, it is the ephemerist, and he almost alone, who records the changing pattern.

Least noticed of all categories of ephemera is the handwritten fragment. Apart from its obvious quality of uniqueness, each item is the direct personal expression of a human experience. Though infinitely fewer and scarcer than printed items, when handwritten ephemera do appear their special qualities make them vastly rewarding. The semi-literate laundry list, the scribbled personal note, the prison-cell appeal for help, the love letter, the threatening note, the begging letter—these are the ephemera of the human condition.

Items of this kind are not to be confused with the letters and documents of the famous. Only rarely do ephemera particularly concern persons of note; their burden is the immediate world of the ordinary man. Today they are the province of a small minority of collectors, but interest is growing, and the next few years will see much useful rescue work.

For collecting purposes, ephemera may be divided into special categories. One specialist will be concerned only with billheads; another with licenses; another with share certificates—and so on. But collections may also ignore these boundaries, concentrating on subject matter rather than kind. A collection illustrating the development of air travel, for example, may incorporate early

passenger tickets, pilots' notes, aircraft blue-prints, flight sched-
ules, bills of lading, joy-ride souvenirs, and a host of dissimilar
but related items. It is in collections like this that the "self-conscious" item—the individual cigarette card, the postcard, or the
postage stamp—may make a welcome contribution.

Any topic may be treated in the same way. Well-established
collecting themes include such varied interests as railways, fashion, crime, airships, medicine, the cinema, public health,
sport, the theater, circuses, and photography. Others less well-
known are bee-keeping, contraception, glassware, cutlery, freedom of the press, footwear, domestic lighting, pen nibs, and sew-
ing machines.

Thematic ephemera collecting normally stems from the collector's existing interests. It is unusual (though not altogether un-
heard-of) for anyone to cast about "looking for something to start
collecting." In general there is a first casual acquisition, then
another and another. Shortly, without formal announcement, a
collection has come into being—a spontaneous expression of its
owner's interest.

Nor, by the way, are collections normally begun as invest-
ments. The typical ephemerist is not, by and large, a tycoon. If
items in his collection appreciate with the passage of time, that is
a peripheral bonus, not the object of the exercise. Normally the
collector is as jealous of unconsidered trifles as he is of major
items. Normally, too, if he parts with anything, he would prefer
to exchange it for other material rather than sell it. He is concerned with ephemera, not with cash returns.

The thematic collection may fulfill a variety of functions. It
may be used in schools as a graphic learning aid; it may be used
in industry to illustrate company history or the development of
special trades and processes. It may outline the growth of a town
or neighborhood, or it may trace the origins of institutions and
organizations. Indeed, the ephemera collection, once the private
foible of the specialist, is now a recognized tool of social history.
It is adaptable to the needs of everyone; the schoolchild may collect items bearing the date of the year of his birth or the current
ephemera of the local High Street; the housewife may gather material to illustrate changing household technology, or inflation, or

the history of fashion, or the development of Women's Lib.

An American businessman collects 19th-Century scholars' reward cards. An English behavioral scientist specializes in 18th- and 19th-Century tradesmen's cards; an art college lecturer collects wartime flagday emblems. A well-known crime writer collects ephemera relating to airships; a London schoolboy collects 19th-Century billheads. The range is endless—and anyone can join in.

2

Our Times in Scraps of Paper

The collector of present-day ephemera requires no guidance on sources. Surrounded on all hands by apparently endless supplies, his job is not to seek but to select. For the packaging specialist the supermarket and the kitchen are hunting-ground enough. For the ticket enthusiast the ordinary day's doings provide their modest quota. Cheese labels, chocolate wrappers, free-gift vouchers, parking tickets, menus, stickers, advertising novelties—the tidal wave of today's ephemera needs no spotlight.

But for the collector of bygones the situation is different. Even to the experienced specialist, the sight of someone else's collection—a tidal wave in miniature—the question springs inevitably: Where do you *get* it all?

The first thing to remember is that, like a bird's nest, no collection is made at a single stroke. Every collection represents the sum total, never quite finished, of innumerable comings and goings. With endless perserevance each individual item is brought home and fitted into the whole. All that is needed is that endless perseverance—and a sharp eye for the individual item.

One good place for the sharp eye to seek ephemera is the antiquarian bookshop. Here, in an odd volume (if you are lucky), you will come across a slipped-in fragment—an ancient ticket, a bill, an advertising card, a shopping list—dropped in on some forgotten day to mark the place. Or you may even find a full-blown bygone bookmark. Or a 19th-Century school report, or a wartime ration card. Or, tucked away on a shelf, an errant pamphlet, a birth certificate, a catalog for an 18th-Century auction, a prospectus for a long-dead gold-mine. Booksellers' shelves, at first sight offering books alone, may nevertheless yield minor trivia. They must be observed minutely: the smallest smitch of protruding paper may indicate a find. The dustiest, most dog-eared corner may be the tip of a collector's piece. *Behind* the books is a good place to look. Crushed and crumpled, items have been known to remain unnoticed for decades.

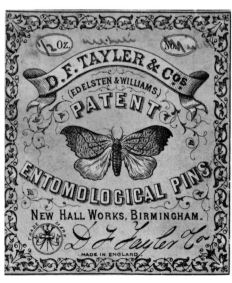

LEFT TO RIGHT, STARTING TOP: TRADE CARD, WATCH PAPER, PRODUCT LABEL, BOOK MAKERS LABEL, BOOKMARK, PIN LABEL—1840-1880

The difficulty—and the advantage—with items of this sort is that long before the browser discovers them, the bookseller has found himself puzzled. The item he has tucked away is not quite his kind of stock-in-trade. Uncertain how best to handle it, he parks it somewhere temporarily. Bookmarks, formal and otherwise, are a problem. Are they part of the book, or cuckoos in the nest? Often the bookman's decision will be in the ephemerist's favor.

In addition to their bookshelf ephemera, most booksellers also maintain an unofficial hideaway where oddments accumulate. Here again, items are preserved "because it seems a shame to throw them away." Tact, and a becoming diffidence, may induce the proprietor to reveal the presence of this *cache* and even to open it up.

Ephemera may also be found in general antiquarian shops. Here, too, it forms a slightly inconvenient sideshow, though attitudes—and prices—may be noticeably more flinty than in the bookshop. Unlike the bookman, the seller of antiques views all items, however miscellaneous, as fair commercial game.

Better by far is the genuine junk shop (particularly the out-of-the-way junk shop) where the field of ephemera remains relatively unexplored. Here, sometimes in surprising abundance, may be found the bundles of unsorted papers that the browser finds it worth his while to acquire on the spot—unbrowsed.

A further source is the print-dealer, among whose stocks of 18th- and 19th-Century engravings ephemera may lurk. But be cause of their exalted context, such items tend to be priced accordingly, even when the seller himself is uncertain of their true value. On the whole it must be said that best ephemera buys do not come much from print sellers.

Also available to the ephemerist as a commercial source is the specialist dealer. Here, too, prices are not low, but the buyer is assured not only of a fair deal but of a selection far wider than the come-by-chance miscellany of the sideshow man.

Happiest hunting-ground of all is the flea-market—the rougher and readier the better. Here it is that newly uncovered ephemera makes a first public appearance. Here is the opportunity of a first sifting. But even here all is not entirely plain sailing. The exhibitor at a flea-market, though he has salvaged the material and brought it to the market himself, may still be inclined to trample it underfoot as he concentrates on his three-dimensionals. On the other hand he may regard a soggy paper compost as "valuable documents." Either way, the going is difficult. Flea-marketing calls for finely-judged diplomacy.

The best source of ephemera are its actual sources—which may, with due circumspection, be discovered. It is after all a matter of finding the right attic, the likely cupboard, the possible valise. With experience, the emphemerist develops a nose for these things. The seach may lead to wild and savage places. Barns, out-houses, abandoned warehouses, lofts and basements, ruined mansions, derelict cottages—with tenacity, and a disregard for dirt and discomfort, these hiding places may yield their hoards.

Patent device for stopping your Horse if he attempts to pass HALE'S Notion Store.
246 Main Street.

ADVERTISING NOVELTY CARD, C. 1880

A well-known collector found a clutch of 19th-Century letterheads as they were about to be baled for pulping at a waste-paper depot. Another snatched a box of 18th-Century parish records from a garbage dump. Another stumbled over a sack of lawyer's throwouts in a vacant office suite.

Garbage men and demolition companies are good to know. Many an important find has been effected through collector/workman teamwork. One such item was the *Lusitania* ticket shown below. (The ticket, bearing the names of a family of five, had survived the sinking though its ill-starred owners had not. It formed part of the evidence in the proceedings brought by next-of-kin, and had come to rest in a London garbage truck in 1972.)

Lawsuit records, and all the papers and scraps that go with them, are a fruitful source of ephemera. As well as wills, deeds, bonds, and other long-forgotten items, each bundle of papers offers its portion of ephemera. No such accumulation is altogether free of old advertising material, business stationery, price lists, trade cards, and unrelated oddments. And to the collector of formal documents—the hard core of legal debris—these throwout bundles are of more than passing interest.

The legal fraternity is of two minds about long-dead records. Professional zeal urges confidentiality and custody; the econom-

ics of space and storage call for disposal. After a generation or two, disposal may win.

It is when a legal practice moves house or closes down that opportunity is at hand for the ephemerist. The sharp-eyed collector is alive to signs of change. Not only the law office, but the local business, the village store, the corner shop, sooner or later clears its decks. Throwing out or selling off may provide a never-to-be-repeated chance. It is at this moment that collector's items may be poised between destruction and rescue.

Another end-of-the-line situation is the formal household auction, where the complete contents of a house, waste-paper and all, may be up for sale. As with the bookseller, again it is ephemera's uncertain status that may provide a collector's bargain. To the auctioneer, more at home with furniture and other momentous items, bundles of paper are often an embarrassment. Here again an unread bundle may be worth the collector's blind bid.

Less frequent, but not to be overlooked, is the chance provided by archive re-arrangement. Libraries, museums, and similar bodies must from time to time review their inventories. Sooner or later, however exalted the body, there has to be a sorting out— sometimes even a whittling down. If the collector is lucky, there may be a slender possibility of fallout. Such occasions are rare, but they have happened.

Also not to be overlooked, as we have noted, is the bulk waste-paper dealer and his customer, the paper-mill proprietor. Somewhere along the line, between baling, carting, storing and the final pulping vat, the ephemerist may contrive a look-in.

The most obviously available source of ephemera, often unrecognized by the newcomer, is the fellow-collector. Every collector is a point of contact with a widening circle of help and information; most will gladly exchange items; many will buy and sell. As a group, they form a mutually helpful look-out service, reporting to each other items of possible interest. It is this characteristic that contributed to the founding of the Ephemera Society, and which has accounted for much of its worldwide success.

But the real first-hand sources, though they require time and effort, remain the best. The lease-end, the removal or the close-down provide opportunities that no amount of shopping around can match. Probably the most productive of all close-downs is the long-established printer. Here, at its very source, may well be the ephemera find of a lifetime. The job printer, as the producer of the material, may serve as the social historian's archive. His files carry specimens of notices, proclamations, advertising throw-aways, leaflets, trade stationery, invitations, tickets and the whole spectrum of neighborhood printed matter. Presented in chronological sequence, without exception and without comment, the printer's file is a history that speaks for itself. To locate such a find, and to rescue it, is the social-history ephemerist's dream.

BLANK PRINTERS TRADE CARD, C. 1885

From just such a file comes the remarkable Soulby Collection, a 30-year record of everyday life of the people of Ulverston, Barrow-in-Furness, at the turn of the 18th Century. Compiled in the course of their daily work by the printers, John Soulby (father) and John Soulby (son), this 700-item collection includes lost-and-found notices, warnings to poachers, summons forms, handbills, trade cards, receipts, price lists, library labels and other items. The collection, housed for the most part in the

Museum of English Rural Life in Reading, presents a uniquely informative picture of its time. Among its many sidelong glances at the affairs of Ulverston is a printed apology from one Richard Cousen, mariner, who "did on Thursday Evening . . . throw a certain Glass Bottle out of the Gallery of the Theatre at Ulverston, to the imminent Danger of the Audience and Performers. . . ." Mr. Cousen is contrite: "I am very sorry for what I did, being in Liquor, and beg this Submission to be Printed and made Public as a Caution to all others. . . ."

As an incidental bonus, the Soulby Collection also records the radical changes in type design that the period produced. Starting in the 1780's with the spindly characters of the early book printers, the collection shows the advent of the "new-style" heavyweight letters, the rumbustious letter-forms of the Victorian sale- and play-bill.

Similar collections, rescued from the debris of yesterday's job printers' workshops, exist elsewhere. The stories of their discovery are ephemerists' classics.

One such story chronicles the Hartlepool find, a rescue in the finest traditions of collectors' treasure trove. Its hero is Robert Wood, ephemerist and citizen of Hartlepool, Lancashire, who early in 1958 happened on a number of spike files in an abandoned building. The files, typical of the record systems of early days, had remained on their spikes for over a hundred years. Their condition was deplorable. Writing of the occasion in a report to fellow-collector Graham Hudson in 1973, Robert Wood described the scene:

"The sight was almost indescribable. Spike files like Christmas trees, black as soot, had been thrown into a large room till it was full to a height of about four feet. Most of the tiles were off the roof and the rain had seeped through above and the plaster of the ceiling had fallen down. To add to the mess, seagulls had nested in the place and there were two or three dead seagulls lying about.

"It was a cold wet windy February morning, so I dragged the nearest file out and took it along the courtyard to the warmth of the boiler house, where I began to peel off the top layers of jet black paper until I could find something readable. Three or four layers down, the paper was clean and I found myself gazing at the proof sheets of the paper railway tickets issued on the Hartlepool Railway in 1837. . . ."

The find decided Robert Wood's spare-time occupation for the next ten years. He spent every available minute extracting and preserving the vast body of material the spikes contained. The papers had belonged to John Procter, who had started in business in Hartlepool in 1834. They included not only file copies of his printing proofs but his personal correspondence and domestic bills.

"All these," writes Robert Wood, "had to be carefully peeled off these sodden piles and sorted out. Obviously it could not be done indoors, and in the short summers I used to sit on my lawn with a spike file before me and two boxes, one on either side, into one of which went what had to be retained, and into the other what I regarded as useless. . . ."

As we picture Robert in his summer garden, happily peeling off layers of Hartlepool history, we have the epitome of the ephemerist in his element.

In forgotten hideaways all over the world such finds still await the enterprising collector. All that is needed is a massive single-mindedness, an unconcern for cleanliness—and a little luck.

3
Search and Rescue

Ephemera need cost the collector nothing at all. For most of the throwaways of our own day—certainly for the Niagara of advertising and promotional material that engulfs us—there is no charge whatsoever. Even with the item that does incidentally involve money, the ticket, the rent demand, the notice to quit or the IOU, the piece of paper itself comes as a bonus—a free gift, with society's compliments. Cheap as it is, it may turn out to be a collector's item.

Present-day ephemera makes its appeal on any or all of a number of counts. It may attract purely as printed design, as souvenir, as history-in-the-making, as curiosity, or simply as an expression of the collector's personal interests.

For the design-conscious, the field is vast. Whether as typographer, graphic designer, printer, publisher, layout man, student of graphics or plain amateur printed-matter-watcher, the design-collector has plenty to choose from. Letterheads, billheads and general business stationery; tickets, invitations, notices, leaflets; packaging and point-of-sale display material; cigar labels, betting slips, lottery tickets, menus, bookmarks, printed serviettes—the list is endless.

In each category the connoisseur discerns the rise and fall of design trends, the changing use of layout and typography. These items mirror exactly the graphic fads and fancies of the day. One distinguished designer has a colorful collection of horse-race betting slips. Another collects orange wrappers. And a lecturer in graphics collects "underground" leaflets and stickers. But design-awareness is by no means confined to experts. For specialist and layman alike the collecting criterion is purely personal: "I collect them because I like them" is the classic comment. A housewife collects printed paper serviettes. A schoolboy collects banana labels. A librarian collects compliment slips. A hospital nurse collects lottery tickets. Each in a short time becomes an expert, a connoisseur in his field. Variants, re-designs, re-issues, "first editions"—all of the finer points of the collector's world apply. So does the lynx-eyed zeal of the hunter. Eye-appeal looms large. At whatever level they appear, most items of ephemera aim to please. Decorative labels, attractively designed promotion items—it is but a step from noticing them in ones and twos to enthusing over them in numbers.

In the souvenir category of ephemera come all those oddments that evoke our yesterdays. Trips abroad, seaside holidays, family jaunts and excursions are all productive of their quota of memorabilia. A complete holiday can be chronicled by its yield of printed miscellany. Tickets, travel folders, price lists, itineraries may bring back, sometimes even more vividly than photographs, the pleasures and adventures of time off. (And we may note in passing that it is not the made-on-purpose souvenir that is necessarily most evocative. Formal souvenirs may not be as evocative for us as our own old luggage tag.)

Other souvenir aspects of ephemera are expressed in neighbor-hood and world-of-my-youth collections. Here the collector gathers local or birth-date items. Among the simplest and quickest to acquire is a complete collection of local shopkeepers' trade cards or billheads. These, assembled over a period of a few weeks or months, may in a very few years acquire considerable local-history interest. Not only does their design and presentation reflect a specific period; the information they convey, in terms of addresses and trading details, may rapidly become matters of history. Changes occur more rapidly than we realize. A complete documentation of a shopping area, perhaps unobtainable from other sources, may form the nucleus of a local-history archive.

Another neighborhood theme could be one's city or town. A single year's output of municipal pamphlets, leaflets and other odds and ends provides a telling expression—easily acquired at the time, but afterwards perhaps unobtainable—of the local social scene.

These items carry a vast amount of factual information on neighborhood affairs, social services and other such matters. Like most ephemera, they also convey a between-the-lines picture of trends and attitudes. An information booklet for the London Borough of Camden has entries on abandoned vehicles, adoption, control of advertising, burials, dental health, pest control,

MODERN EPHEMERA

drains, elderly persons, factory inspection—and so on through to unmarried mothers, vaccination, water safety, and workshops for the handicapped.

World-of-my-youth items of ephemera, only slightly more difficult to come by, make a special appeal to the younger collector. The ephemerist gathers material dating, for example, from the first year, or the first decade, of his life. Here again, in a quickly changing world, the very recent bygone may gain remarkably in interest as each year passes. For the ten-year-old collector the newspaper front pages that appeared on the day of his birth may convey a world of unimaginable remoteness. So too the election campaign material, the price lists, the student sit-in literature, the charred draft-card and the Common Market "NO" sticker.

The category of "curiosity" ephemera, more specialized than others, and requiring greater tenacity, can be no less rewarding. Here the criterion is mere quirkiness—an appeal to the collector's personal sense of the odd, the ridiculous or amusing. One specialist collects incomprehensible instruction leaflets. Another has an eye for the quirky notice. (A catering exhibition displaying fine foods carried notices saying "Please do Not Eat the Exhibition.") Yet another collects examples of fractured phrases on foreign products: "Close the point of contact with a humid stuff, in order that the steam goes up to the couscous."

Another collector specializes in computerized accountancy

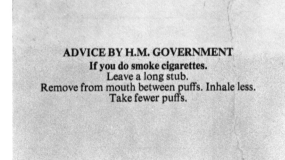

ADVICE BY H.M. GOVERNMENT
If you do smoke cigarettes.
Leave a long stub.
Remove from mouth between puffs. Inhale less.
Take fewer puffs.

BENSON & HEDGES CIGARETTE CARD. 1975

claims for gigantic sums for electricity bills. Another has a world collection of refuse-men's Christmas cards. These, in their respective languages, are mailed or left with householders as a hint as gift time draws near.

Further offbeat collectibles include editors' rejection slips, telegram forms, summonses, final demands, ships' newspapers, lodging-house tickets, misprints, and printed toilet paper.

Among only-just-bygone ephemera (now, alas, not available free of charge) are the colorful crate labels, till recently inseparable from fruit and vegetable marketing; and hotel and resort labels, the promotional stickers that only a short while ago mysteriously appeared on travelers' luggage. Equally evocative and only just not contemporary are record jackets from the 78 rpm era; one collector has amassed some fifteen hundred of these newly nostalgic items.

A huge field for the collector of present-day ephemera is packaging. All over the world the supply and acquisition of packaged produce is a major activity, and the all-important containers in which this material is conveyed to the consumer form an industry in themselves. But, vital as they are, packages normally vanish without trace. Ironically, these most universal of items are among the least documented. With one or two notable exceptions among specialized collectors, their history has been neglected. The ecologist may cry for a halt in the tide of packaging (as well for a halt to throwaways in general) but there seems no valid reason why history should wholly ignore it.

The package collector points to the obvious gaps in our knowledge of yesterday's shopping scene. Packages, such as they may have been, were destroyed—virtually on delivery. The early printed carton or wrapper, undamaged and in mint condition, is today a rarity. So it will be with today's generation, says the collector, if no consistent effort is made to preserve specimens for the record. Thus it is that Robert Opie, possibly the world's leading packaging collector, includes among his collection not only yesterday's packs but a vast contingent of today's. "Posterity will be relieved to know," he says, "that there are now three thousand different yogurt cartons in my collection awaiting its appraisal."

It is in the area of social-history record that collectors of present-day ephemera stand strongest. Whatever the charms of graphic design, of curiosities, personal souvenirs and misprints, the long-term value of today's material is in its implicit chronicle of the times. The social-history collector concentrates on subject matter, regardless of form or category. A collection on a given theme may include items as disparate as a sticker and a government proclamation, a bookplate and a honey jar label.

For the most part, not surprisingly, it is the major issues reflected by historical ephemera that claim attention. Urban violence, contraception, inflation, race equality—these are typical of the more obvious themes that today's ephemera may illustrate. Less obvious, but no less readily depicted, are such subjects as illiteracy, the changing church, medical ethics, computerization, radioactivity, worker participation in industry. The thoughtful ephemerist takes his choice.

At the Ephemera Society's opening exhibition in London in 1975, a complete panel was devoted to a random display of present-day material. It showed, among other items, the following:

Kidney-donor's consent card.

Notice warning office workers to be on the alert for letter-bombs.

Ticket of admission to a lodging-house.

Waldorf-Astoria room card with the headline "Thou shalt not tempt," advising visitors not to leave valuables unprotected.

Anti-abortion leaflet giving details of short-stay hostels for unmarried mothers-to-be.

Package of cigarettes supplied "for the exclusive use of officers and men of the Royal Navy," and bearing the Government warning "Smoking can damage your health."

"SAC" newsheet—journal of the Squatters' Action Council.

Computerized invoice, from the Massachusetts Institute of Technology Press, in which the final amount to pay is entered as "00.00."

Leaflet in Greek issued by the Borough of Camden for the Cypriot community. Subject: Backgammon Contest.

Printed card from American Express advising restaurant keepers of numbers of defaulting cardholders.

NOT TO BE TAKEN AWAY

𝔚estminster 𝔄bbey

AIR RAID WARNINGS

Should an Air Raid warning be sounded during Service the procedure to be adopted is as follows :—

1. All Abbey doors (except the East Cloister door) will be open.

2. The Service will at once be closed with the Blessing or the Grace.

3. In view of their special A.R.P. duties the Choir will leave the Abbey with all reverent speed and proceed to their posts of duty.

4. The congregation are urged also to leave the Abbey and take cover in the Shelters provided in the basement of the Methodist Central Hall, or in the basement of the new Church House at south side of Dean's Yard.

5. The Clergy and Vergers on duty will remain in the Abbey until the congregation have had an opportunity to leave.

N.B.—The Public are advised that the Abbey is not a safe place during an Air Raid—and are strongly advised to take shelter as recommended above at any time when an Air Raid warning is given.

PAUL DE LABILLIERE,
Dean.

October, 1939   Vacher 69638

• 31 •

Shareholder's printed return-envelope addressed to "Rolls-Royce Limited (In Voluntary Liquidation)."

"Free Ticket" issued by Widow Brown's Inn "in the heart of beautiful downtown Stockertown. It's not good for anything, it's just free."

Sticker bearing an image of a gun and the slogan "All workers should read the monthly Irish Liberation Press."

Post Office notice warning that "mail left unattended in the public office will be treated as suspect and disposed of accordingly."

Restaurant menu announcing price increases.

Police appeal to Scottish mountaineers to leave details of their proposed route in case of emergency.

Ticket of admission to view Salisbury Cathedral.

New York hotel notice: "No bare feet allowed."

Sticker: "Join the Army, see the world, meet interesting new people and kill them."

Notice: "Crime scene search area. STOP. No admittance beyond this point until search is completed.
                              Police Department, New York."

Notice: "Store Detectives Operating."

Notice: "No Dogs Admitted—except guide dogs for the blind."

Welcome to The Waldorf-Astoria
Park Avenue between 49th and 50th Streets
New York, N.Y. 10022

Thou Shalt Not Tempt!

Please do not leave money, travelers checks or jewelry unprotected in your room — we are not responsible for valuables unless checked. Safe Deposit Boxes are available in the Lobby Office at no charge. "Thank You"

The Management

FRUIT CRATE LABEL, C. 1950

Marcus McCorison, Director of the American Antiquarian Society in Worcester, Massachusetts, has aptly described ephemera as a "window into the center of a culture." The phrase is valid for contemporary specimens as it is for bygones.

Present-day items of ephemera cost little or nothing; taken individually, they are often too insignificant to attract much notice; they are in the main so common that nobody normally thinks of preserving them. They are produced, by common consent, to be thrown away. It is in this very quality of triviality and transience that their potential value lies. Salvaged, and presented coherently, they form part of a story that speaks for itself.

In 1977 a call went out for items for a commemorative display featuring the 1951 Festival of Britain. All that was required was minor ephemera, a few examples from among the many millions of items that the event had generated. To the nation's surprise, little or nothing had survived. It had been so common at the time, everyone had thrown it away.

Royal Opera House
COVENT GARDEN
Opera - Cosi Fan Tutte
EVENING 7-30
THURSDAY, NOVEMBER 4
ORCH. STALLS
£8·80 Incl. VAT
To be retained
Conditions see over G 28

4

Business Bygones

Few categories of ephemera convey the image of their time more vividly than business stationery. The bygone letterhead, or billhead, with its graphic presentation of product or shop or factory; the price list, the trade card, the receipt—these, as well as showing the trade and business of the past, record details of actual transactions, actual goods or services bought and sold by actual people. They are also, as it happens—at least in their more recent forms—among the most readily acquired of yesterday's collector's items. In neglected drawers and cupboards the business stationery of the early 20th Century is still to be found in handfulls. These revealing fragments, till recently largely ignored, now come into their own as social documents.

Not least of their attractions is their stress on visual presentation of premises. Garlanded in scrollwork and elaborate lettering, perspectives of works and warehouses assure us of the substance of the enterprise. Through a magnifier we observe the detail. Horse-drawn drays and wagons trundle in and out of factory gates while chimneys billow and workers load and unload materials. Outside the gates, respectable couples, she with a bustle, he with a bowler and cane, pursue their strolling progress, their heads turned in appreciation of the scene.

In the never-never world of letterhead engraving, all is productivity, order and admiration. We may be sure that it was not really quite like that, but doubtless like enough to pass for real.

The graphic idiom of these designs sprang apparently from nowhere. It was born some time in the 1870's and flourished furiously, lingering in patches till as late as the 1930's and '40's. (Even in the 1970's, one or two firms remain faithful to their scrolls and curlicues—complete with telephone and telex numbers.) The style, while it overlapped the period of *art nouveau,* was yet distinct—a design world of its own, confined almost entirely to commercial stationery.

But these elaborate creations were only the latest in a long tra-

LETTERHEAD, 1895

dition of letter- and billheads. For its forebears we go back to the early tradesman's card, the origin of all business stationery, and indeed the origin of most forms of commercial printed matter.

The "trade card," as it came to be called, evolved almost by accident. It was actually not a card at all, but a smallish piece of paper with an engraving of the trademan's name printed on it. It was an all-purpose item. It was sometimes used to carry a customer's account, sometimes as a jotter for notes or prices or instructions to messengers. It might also be used as a promotion leaflet, or even, if it were pasted up somewhere, as a small poster.

Trade cards had come into general use as a substitute for the shopkeeper's hanging sign. These, because of their proliferation (and because of their danger to the populace in high winds) had been done away with in the 1760's. The image on the sign—a boot, a hat, or whatever other product—now appeared on the slip

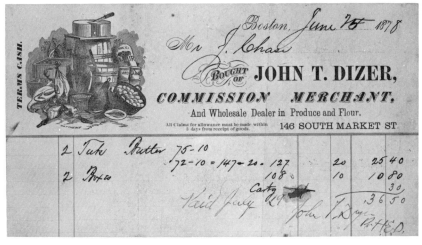

BILLHEAD, 1878

of paper. There were also instructions on how to find the place of business ("Over against the Royal Exchange, near the church-yard"). When street numbering began, also in the 1760's, the number was added or substituted.

Though they were later to become in fact cards (eventually the business card as we know it today) trade cards remained in the form of paper throwaways for over a century.

The several uses of the term, "trade card," have resulted in much confusion—compounded in modern times by the use of the term to describe cards given with tea, chocolate and other such products. (These, specifically produced as collectibles and de-vised, like cigarette cards, to increase sales, are not trade cards at all. The term, "trade card," relates only to the true business card: a presentation, illustrated or otherwise, of the nature of a product or service, the name of the proprietor, and his address.)

The trade card, first appearing in Britain about 1630, was until the turn of the 18th Century almost the only generally recognized form of commercial advertising. Into it was packed all the infor-mation—and all the prestigious atmosphere—that the tradesman sought to convey. Trade-cards designers and engravers (among them such distinguished names as Bartolozzi and Hogarth) were members of an artist-craftsman elite. Their clients, who ranged from purveyors of luxuries to His Majesty to specialists in the dis-posal of domestic sewage, relied on them for the projection of an elegant image. They were the true precursors of the advertising man.

As with today's practitioners, the makers of trade cards were enthusiastic to the point of excess. But their idiom, unlike to-day's, which ordinarily seeks the broadest appeal, was geared specifically to the taste of the upper classes. These, the only sec-tors of the public affluent enough to afford the advertised ser-vices, were the trade cards' target.

Thus it is that we see on trade cards the use of devices, visual and editorial, designed to catch the eye of the gentry. Coats of arms (above all, the coveted "Royal Appointment"), flourishes and curlicues abound. So does elegant, and often obsequious, language: "Williams, Crediton, respectfully solicits the kind pa-tronage of the Nobility and Gentry . . . and hopes by Assiduity

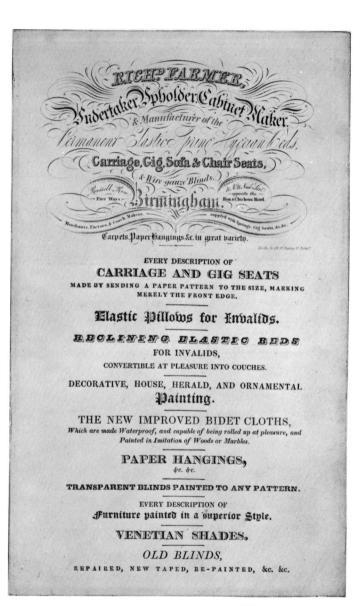

EVERY DESCRIPTION OF

CARRIAGE AND GIG SEATS

MADE BY SENDING A PAPER PATTERN TO THE SIZE, MARKING
MERELY THE FRONT EDGE.

Elastic Pillows for Invalids.

RECLINING ELASTIC BEDS

FOR INVALIDS,

CONVERTIBLE AT PLEASURE INTO COUCHES.

DECORATIVE, HOUSE, HERALD, AND ORNAMENTAL

Painting.

THE NEW IMPROVED BIDET CLOTHS,

*Which are made Waterproof, and capable of being rolled up at pleasure, and
Painted in Imitation of Woods or Marbles.*

PAPER HANGINGS,
&c. &c.

TRANSPARENT BLINDS PAINTED TO ANY PATTERN.

EVERY DESCRIPTION OF

Furniture painted in a superior Style.

VENETIAN SHADES.

OLD BLINDS,

REPAIRED, NEW TAPED, RE-PAINTED, &c. &c.

TRADE CARD, 1820-1830

and Attention to merit a Continuance of their Support."

These classic phrases, first formulated by some unknown consultant in the mists of the 17th Century, became fixed as standard trade copy. They persisted at least into the 1890's.

The trade card reveals much marginal information on trade and industry in general. Not least of its revelations is the multiplicity of services and products often supplied by a single tradesman. A typical "multiple" appears in a card from the famous collection of Dr. Anthony Ambrose: H. Jackson, of Rathbone Place, London, is described not only as "auctioneer, appraiser and upholder" but as "undertaker, cabinet, chair and sofa manufacturer." Other versatile operators combined "patent medicines and account books" and similarly ill-assorted products.

Trade cards may often supply important information on early inventions and processes. The collection of scientific trade cards housed in the Science Museum, London, serves as a source of science history, showing which supplier first introduced, manufactured or modified given instruments—sometimes even indicating their original inventor. (The cards also reveal that spectacle makers went from house to house with their wares: "Mr. Morris will call with a large assortment. . . . This bill will be called for. . . .").

The use of the word "bill" on trade cards is a pointer to the de-

CHROMO-LITHO TRADE CARD, C. 1880

veloping role of the card. It did service as a bill of account, a handbill, and a "billpqster's bill." The original engraved plate was printed at the head of a plain sheet as an account, and later as a letterhead. The plate also had an extended use in local trade directories. The image was printed centrally on an otherwise blank page to form part of the advertisement section

The trade card, at first a minor document, became the father and mother of all printed publicity. It is a central item in the history of commerce.

For the collector the early trade card in its various forms provides insights at a variety of levels. It reflects the development of trade, of social attitudes, of design trends and of printing techniques. It is also, apart from these characteristics, an object of great visual charm. The trade card has in recent years become a much-prized item. Unlike the turn-of-the-century billhead, it is now scarce and relatively costly. But still, with luck, trade cards continue to emerge from forgotten bales and bundles. They are well worth hunting for.

The engraved trade card, with its single-color image (mostly black), was followed in the latter part of the 19th Century by the brightly colored chromo-litho card—an item of a very different kind. Of these, many thousands survive.

The chromo-litho trade card stands in much the same relation to its forerunner as color to monochrome television. The chromo-litho process, with its ability to reproduce the liveliest—and the subtlest—of color gradations, quite vanquished the old black-and-white tradition. Gone, almost overnight, was 18th Century elegance; in its place came the most vigorous of polychrome pictorialism, harbinger of the full-color magazine advertisement and the color poster. It was in America that the chromo-litho trade card flourished. Brought from its birthplace by German immigrants, popular lithography swamped the market. Instead of devising his own card, the tradesman (now called "the advertiser") used pre-printed designs supplied for overprinting with his name and message. In vast quantities these decorative cards were bought by shopkeepers and manufacturers throughout the land.

In the great majority of cases the pictorial element on chromo-litho trade cards bore no relation to the subject matter. The cards were simply pleasing "picture cards," produced often in sets with a view to being collected. With this transformation the trade card lost its innocence; it had become advertising.

Hard on the heels of the new concept came the meat-extract and chocolate manufacturers with specially produced sets of cards for collectors. ("Liebig" cards, now being assiduously re-collected, are typical.) Here the trade card had finally lost its identity.

Toward the end of the 19th Century the commercial picture-card idea was extended to scholars' reward cards (a convention existing, without benefit of advertising, since the early 1800's) and to cigarette cards. These last, initially inserted as blank package stiffeners, became a minor medium in their own right, in Britain conveying potted information to millions.

Second cousin to the colored trade card was the magazine insert. These, however, had no pretensions to educational virtue. Resembling miniature posters, they were designed to be bound in with the popular magazines of the day as straightforward advertising matter. (Today's survivors more often than not show damage to the disbound edge, though a minority, used as counter leaflets, remain unscathed.) With the coming of the magazine insert the full transition from shopkeeper's name-card to manufacturer's publicity was complete.

Collections of any or all of these items in the development of the trade card, either as separate categories or as cross-fertilizing streams in the evolution of publicity, convey their genealogy clearly. They show the whole extraordinary story of the move from the individual craftsman to industrialization, from the family business to mass production. They form an epitome of one of the most significant periods of human history.

Not least among the archives of commerce—and also stemming from the trade card—is the price list. Here, in reliable detail, are the actual facts and figures of yesterday's shopping, statistical raw material for economist and social historian alike. The price list, though it was to grow into an item in its own right, was originally an addendum to the trade card, sometimes appearing as a handwritten memo, later as a printed statement, on the front

IMPORTANT 29 Aug.t 186

To the Inhabitants of Homerton

B. ROEBUCK

Respectfully informs his Friends and the Public generally that he intends OPENING on SATURDAY EVENING NEXT the Premises situate at

No 1, Crozier's Terrace

Near the "Spread Eagle,"

HOMERTON,

IN THE

GROCERY

And General Line,

Where he hopes by strict attention to Business and supplying Articles of Superior Quality at the Lowest possible Prices to secure their liberal support.

B. R. also informs the Inhabitants that he intends to supply them with

Fresh Pork, Ready Dressed Ham and Beef, &c.

N.B.—TABLE BEER of a Superior Quality.

PLEASE OBSERVE THE ADDRESS

1, CROZIER'S TERRACE, HOMERTON.

ADVERTISING LEAFLET, 1863

or back of the card. Specialist collectors may concentrate on price lists from particular trades or industries; others may collect general lists from specific economic periods. As with other ephemera, the price list provides information that may otherwise be difficult or impossible to trace.

A further fertile source of commercial history is the advertising leaflet. This, too, is a close relation to the trade card, coming into popular use in the early 1800's. It was handed out in the streets and was slipped under doors. It had the distinction of being the first clearly identifiable form of publicity hand-out nuisance.

Unlike the trade card, which was the product of expert artist/engravers, the leaflet was produced by the relatively untutored (and sometimes barely literate) job printer. It was directed not to the gentry but to the man in the street. It pulled no punches. In layout, phraseology, and psychological approach, the leaflet reflected a level of society previously unexpressed in print. But it still could not resist a hint of the air of its forebears. A rag, bone and bottle merchant, soliciting among other things old boots and shoes, broken flint glass, horse hair and dripping, writes that he "respectfully informs the inhabitants of this and the surrounding neighbourhood that he has just taken these premises, where he hopes by adhering to his old principles of strict attention, Civility, Just Weight, and Giving the Highest Possible Price for every article, to be favoured by a large share of the patronage which it will always be his endeavour to merit."

Shopkeepers' paper bags and wrapping paper provide yet another view of the commercial scene. These items ranged from the smallest squares for dispensing snuff, tobacco and confectionery, to grocers' and bakers' bags and, later in the last century, tear-off wrapping rolls. All were printed with the tradesman's name and many carried illustrations—some of no small merit. Here, too, the series idea emerged; some tobacconists' wrappers carried jingles, jokes or conundrums; bakers' bags showed views of well-known beauty spots. The collecting idea, with its concomitant of repeated purchases, was never far away.

Paper bags and wrappers found their logical conclusion in the development of packaging. With the advent of mass production, packing, display, and promotion of commodities passed from storekeeper to manufacturer. The coming of the branded product brought to the package a role not merely as container but as banner-bearer. Into its design went all the arts and devices of the emerging advertising industry. Today's collections of packaging recount the story of the rise of mass market; so do the display cards, counter containers, and promotional novelties that went with it. Most of these items, were it not for the rescue work of the collector, would have vanished without trace.

Last, and possibly the most significant field of commercial ephemera, is the poster. A direct descendant of the trade card, the poster is the small-scale chromo-litho card writ large. Here too, with intelligent selection, we have a vehicle for the narration of social history. The story of an industry—an epoch, a national campaign, a war, a revolution—may be told through chronological presentation of poster images.

The great collections of posters, such as those in the Victoria and Albert Museum and the Library of Congress, are too often viewed as collections of "marginal art." They are very much more than that: they are records in the story of human affairs. The private collector, no less than the great institutions, may share in the shaping of the records.

LETTER BOMB WARNING

WATCH OUT FOR

SMALL PACKETS BEARING AN UNUSUAL POSTMARK

WATCH OUT FOR

UNFAMILIAR HANDWRITING OR INCORRECT SPELLING AND TITLES

WATCH OUT FOR

ANY SMALL BOOKS ARRIVING

DON'T

MOVE ANY STRANGE OR SUSPICIOUS LETTERS OR PACKETS

DON'T

DROP THE LETTER IN WATER

DON'T

TRY TO OPEN THE ENVELOPE WITH A PAPER KNIFE OR LETTER OPENER

DON'T

SHAKE IT OR SQUEEZE IT

DO

ISOLATE IT

DO

EVACUATE THE ROOM AND ALERT ALL STAFF

DO RING THE FIREMEN EXT. 222

REMEMBER
LEAVE ALONE ANY SUSPICIOUS LETTER PACKET OR PARCEL

LONDON POSTER, 1976

5

Everyday Throwaways

The collector of ephemera may approach the matter from one of two ways—sometimes from both at once. He may collect by *category* or *theme*. He may concentrate, for example, on the category of chromo-litho trade cards, regardless of their theme. Or he may focus, for example, on education (or phrenology, or motoring, or horticulture or whatever) taking in ephemera in any category provided they relate to his subject.

A category collection will show a certain tidy uniformity; a theme collection will not. Trade cards fit fairly neatly within given physical limits; a collection on the theme of education may contain items as disparate as a child's reward card, a school report, and a broadside announcing classes in double-entry bookkeeping. The thematic collector has a wide field to choose from. Ephemera may illustrate virtually any subject or interest; the formation of a collection is a matter of personal taste and—within the chosen field—discriminating selection.

In the matter of a theme, the aspirant's own interests will generally be his best guide. But, for the record, below is a random list of themes, many of them the subject of existing ephemera collections, some of them recently started, some in contemplation. (No one, by the way, should be diffident about the possibility of "duplicating" someone else's collection; in every field the potential is so vast that no two collectors are ever likely to suffer more than the mildest of overlap.)

Education	Church	Optics
Public health	Electricity	Space
Medicine	Coal	Tramways
Railways	Dancing	Buses
Hotels	Law	Motor cars
Travel	Turnpikes	Sport
Coaching	Theater	Birth control
Poor law	Cookery	Music hall
Prisons	Needlework	Candles

TRADE CARD, C. 1890

Workhouse	Cutlery	Charity
Taxation	Cosmetics	Music
Hygiene	Airships	Magic lantern
Radio	Wool	Insurance
Gambling	Employment	Cinema
Warfare	Restaurants	Game laws
Revolution	Domestic science	Crime
Hospitals	Police	Gas
Circuses	Dentistry	Silk
Libraries	Horse transport	Drink
Aircraft	Superstition	Newspapers
Footwear	Phrenology	Steam
Glass	Obstetrics	Agriculture
Perfume	Quack medicine	Fairs
Pharmaceuticals	Auctioneering	Funerals
Banking	Parachuting	Deaf-mutes
Palmistry	Surgery	Punch and Judy
Fashion	Shipping	Tithes
Prohibition	Gardening	Conjuring
Printing	Canals	Cotton
Vaccination	Navy	Oil
Travel	Slavery	Shops

To see how the thematic principle works out, we may examine a few of the items in a typical collection.

Example 1:

Theme: *"The Golden Age of the Horse"*

Way-bill of the Harvard & Groton Accommodation Coach, showing passengers' names, fares and destinations. 1842.

Notebook containing blacksmith's accounts. 1833—34.

Label: "Alterative or Condition Powders for Horses" ("Give a tablespoon every day in damped corn.") 1860.

Trade card: Stocken & Storey (Patentee of "a step for more easy access into and upon high carriages.") 1865.

Tax form showing annual assessment for male servants, carriages, armorial bearings. 1882.

Invoice: "Coach hire to St. James Square, back to Temple Bar, Back to Park Street, Westminster, then Back: 14 shillings." 1830.

Leaflet: "Needham's Portable Spurs. . . .Decidedly the most convenient that have been made, being put on and taken off in an instant, and are so portable that they may be carried in the waistcoat pocket. . . ." 1850.

Cab ticket, Paris. 1860.

Printed announcement: "A Proposal for Procuring Travelling Partners at Short Notice" (obviating the need for a solitary passenger to pay for an empty seat as well as his own in a two-seat post chaise). 1777.

Letterhead: "The HP Horse Nail Company." 1879.

Police notice: "To owners and drivers of carts and other conveyances" forbidding riding on the shaft, driving on the wrong side of the road, driving more than two carts at once, driving a carriage without name and address of owner painted on it, etc. 1841.

Leaflet: Weekly Removal of Stable Manure." Reminder from town clerk, Accrington, concerning by-laws. 1913.

Children's board game label: "Jeu de Tramway" showing horse tram. circa 1880.

Label: "Remedy for foot rot." circa 1900.

Letterhead: "Manhattan Horse Manure Company. Gatherers, Dealers and Shippers of Manure." 1912.

Trade card (misprint): "Farmer & Jenkins . . . BLCKSMITHS, Goffstown, N. H. . . Shoeing promptly attended to . . . ." 1910.

Trade card: "John Gulliver's apprentice (Polo) has open a Shop to himself and he is determined to give every satisfaction to every gentleman that may favour him with a Trial and he will shoe Horses for 3 shillings per set he served a faithful apprenticeship of 7 years to his master. N.B. He works for the Officers of the 57th Regiment." 1850.

Hackney cabman's contract with cab proprietor, London. 1858.

It will be seen, even from this sketchy outline of just a few items in the collection, that the material presents a graphic impression of its subject matter. (It may also be noted, by the way, that most of the items were acquired in flea-markets at a cost hardly greater than that of thirty or forty cigarettes.)

Example 2:
Theme: *Shipping*

Booklet: "How to Obtain Berths on the Large Liners": Advice to aspiring employees. "Buglers assist deck steward and blow before meals." 1904.

Certificate of Health: Issued by authorities in Oporto to ship bound for London. ". . . by the Divine Mercy of God, this City is free from the Pestilence. . . ." 1828.

Marine insurance policy: ". . .touching the Adventures and Perils. . .of the Sea, Men of War, Fire, Enemies, Pirates, Rovers, Thieves, Jettisons. . . Surprisals." etc. 1858.

Share certificate: "The Great Ship Company" (Brunel's *Great Eastern*). 1859.

Regulations for Maintaining Discipline: Penalties for offences, including "Interrupting Divine Service by indecorous Conduct—fined one day's pay; Swearing or using Improper Language—fined one day's pay; Neglecting to bring up, open out and air bedding when ordered—fined half a day's pay; Washing clothes on a Sunday—one day's pay; (For the Cook) Not having any meal of the Crew ready at the appointed time—one day's pay." etc. 1855.

Bill of lading: "Shipped by the Grace of God in Good Order and well conditioned. . .in and upon the good Ship called the

Adriana. . . Bound for Philadelphia . . . . 3 Chests & 1 Bale of Merchandise. . . . And so God send the good Ship to her desired Port in Safety—Amen." 1781

Notebook entry, handwritten: "Charles Connard, aged 18. Born 30 September 1789. Went to sea the 10th of April 1804. Lost in January 1807."

Receipt: "For towage from sea to city [New Orleans], Packet rate $250." 1836.

Damage report: Voyage from Cuba to Portland: "Eighteen boxes of sugar more or less wet. . . . Some of the boxes are in a liquid state. . . ." 1867.

Sale agreement: "The schooner *Bulla,* built in Jersey, 1873 . . .for the sum of One Thousand and Fifty Pounds. . . ." 1878.

Leaflet: Ostend/Dover mail steamers, "Caution. In their own interests, passengers are requested (1) not to play at cards with strangers, (2) to beware of pickpockets." 1913.

Example 3:
Theme: *The Poor*

Inventory: "Stock of provisions, clothes, linen, flannel and other goods in Liverpool Workhouse." The list includes picked oakum, wood bowls, noggins, trenchers, tin bowls and spitting cans, coffins, drugs, oil, leeches, etc. 1820.

Letter (to the Trustees of Windsor Almshouses): "Gentlemen: I shall be pleased to supply bread for the almshouses at 4½ pence per 4 lb. loaf for the next 12 months. . . ." circa 1870.

Warrant: "Watt's Charity [Rochester, Kent]. This warrant admits the bearer to the Traveller's Hall, on the right-hand side of the entrance, and is an order for a Night's Lodging, which with Fourpence, is conformable to the will of the late Richard Watts, Esquire. . . . The additonal comfort of fire and candle is given during the Winter months, i.e. from 18th October, until 10th March. . . ." 1831.

Information (part printed) to the Overseers of the Poor of the Town of Bristol from the Overseers of the Poor for Hallowell, 1842. "Gentlemen: Leonard Peters, a reputed child of Hannah Dick by Benjamin Peters, an inhabitant of your town, has now become chargeable in this town as a pauper. We conceive it necessary to give you this information, and to request that you order his removal, or otherwise provide for him as you would judge expedient. We have charged the expense of his support, which has already arisen, to your town, and shall continue to do so, so long as we are obliged to furnish him with supplies. . . ." 1842.

Selectmen's Report: "Caleb Coolidge, aged 56, Bording at Doc^r Ball at 3 dollars per week for Eight weeks to the 4th of January 1808 and 5 dollars per week to the 17th of February 1808. From that date til he went to live with his son Henry Coolidge at Westmester for one year at one dollar Per week the Town to be at the Expense of doctring and Clothing."

Printed form: "Mr. Provider: Please to relieve this poor Traveller with Four-pence. . . ." 1773.

Appeal card: "No father! No mother!! To the Governors and Subscribers of the Merchant Seamen's Orphan Asylum. . . the favour of your Vote and Interest is most earnestly solicited on the behalf of Isabella Wilson Whose Father was Chief Mate in the John Bushman, a Baltic Trader, and died from the effects of Shipwreck, leaving three Orphan Children to the entire care of an aged Grandfather (who is a Widower) and entirely unable to support such a charge; their Mother having previously died. . . ." circa 1830.

Constable's bill (to the Overseers of the Poor "of the township of Darlington" from Thomas Littlefair, Constable): "Removing Margaret Nelson and her 2 children to Northallerton under Order of Removal, Convaince from Darting to Northallerton 7/6d; Dinner at Northallerton 1/6d; Convaince from Northallerton to Darlington 1/7d; One day at 3 shillings per day 3/-. . . ."

Apprentice indenture, made between the Overseers of the Poor of the Borough of Lancaster and William Mason, Gentleman, for the placing of John Waddington, "a poor boy of this Borough . . . of the Age of 10 years or thereabouts' apprentice with Mason." The agreement binds the apprentice to good behaviour: ". . . at Cards, Dice, or any unlawful Game, he shall not Play. . . . Ale-houses, Taverns, evil Company he shall not frequent. . . . Fornication or Adultery he shall not commit, nor Matrimony contract, during the said Term. . . ." 1780.

These rescued oddments, most of them acquired by chance or by flea-market diligence, conspire to paint a memorable picture. Each separate item, perhaps less significant on its own, takes on a fuller meaning in context with its neighbors. Within a short while the whole collection becomes greater than the sum of its parts.

For the thematic collector of ephemera, anything that is relevant is grist to the mill; for the category collector, life may seem slightly less multifarious. Once he has settled his terms of reference, there are only two decisions to be made on anything he may come across: does it, or does it not, come within his category? If it does, does he like it? The rest is simple.

The preliminary decision matters most. Which category to settle for? A short list, over and above the commercial material mentioned in the last section, might include lottery tickets, library labels, bookmarks, banknotes, passports, share certificates, deeds, calendars, music covers, board games, insurance policies, summonses, bills of lading, taxation papers, notices to quit, indentures, programs, magazines, newspapers, draft cards, school reports, menus, permits, proclamations, notices, labels, touring maps, instruction sheets, aerial leaflets, price tags, dance cards, election badges, scholars' reward cards, checks, book and record tokens, calling cards, ration cards, auction catalogs, battle orders, betting slips, folk recipes, licenses, greeting cards, scraps, timetables, tickets, invitations, compliment slips, telegram forms, final demands, mourning cards, car stickers and many more.

Each of these special categories of ephemera has its own experts, its own folklore, its finer points and its own scene-stealers. Each is a collecting world of its own, but each is open to everyone. Each sector is also susceptible of thematic sub division: the label specialist may focus only on chemists' labels—or needle or button or nib or perfume or stationers' or tea or perfume or cigar or pin-packet labels. The tax-fancier may favor tax forms for assessments on land, manservants, hair powder, armorial bearings, horses, salt or windows. The ticket man may ignore all institutions other than railways—or theaters, or sports events, or concerts.

There is no limit to the potential fineness of the ephemerist's focus. He is his own master. He makes his own rules and—mostly—sticks to them.

6
Fragments in Pen and Ink

Hitherto neglected, items of handwritten ephemera now begin to take their rightful place alongside their printed neighbors. Though the collector of printed material may at first look askance at pen and ink, brief acquaintance with part-printed, part-written items such as receipts and forms may tend to modify his view.

It becomes apparent that many significant specimens carry only the smallest ingredient of print; their value may lie overwhelmingly in their handwritten content. A craftsman's invoice is no less valid, and no less of a social-history record, if the written entries outshine his printed name and address. Nor, by the same token, if the printed element is absent altogether.

The handwritten fragment—the laundry list, the charwoman's receipt, the scribbled note—these are part of society's heritage, visible evidence of the everyday lives of ordinary people. They stand in the same relationship to formal manuscripts and autographs as printed ephemera stand to books. They are fugitive and important.

If printed ephemera provides an insight into the life of mankind, how very much more direct is the view provided by these personal pen-to-paper records of real people. To an increasing number of ephemerists they are subjects of search and rescue.

Consider this, an appeal to a parish church for help after a fire in London's East End in 1792:

> Honoured Ladys and Gentlemen
> I Begg Leave to inform you of my melencoly Misforten which hapened to me the 25 Aprile at 2.0 Clock in the morning I being a sleep in Thomas Beadles house in Rudman Lane in the parish of St. george In the east the house was all on fire Before I was alarmed and I run to save my Life with my Shift and nightcape and leaft My all behind me which was almost seven Pounds of monney and wearabels so that I am In great misery and has nothing to support me With so I hope that you will Remember Us all in mercy, this is all from your humble Pettishener
>> Eleanor Lockhart

Consider this, too—a plea to the magistrate from a parish apprentice in 1876:

> Sir
>
> Mr Bennetts Brother as struck me once & he is allways swearing at Me & he said the Other Day that he would Kick me they have acused me of taking things he is such a violent Temper that I am afraid he will turn me off the Ladder some day when my Father Spoke to Mr Bennett about Apprenticing me he ask[d] Mr Bennett if he could take me to learn the Pluming trade he as so little to do that there is no chance of my learning the Trade i am Generaly at work with Mr Bennetts Brother he is by trade a Hatter they make me wash coal carts and Paint them i am running for Errands & mooving tools from the shop to Different Jobbs and Back Mr Bennetts Brother sent me home Last week & Stop[d] some of my Pay when he sent me home Last week he swore at me & told me he would kick me behind i had an accident some time Back & Mr Bennett stop[d] half my wages for 6 Weeks Gentlemen I should be thankful if you would cancell My Indenture & allow me to get another Master where i may have the chance of Learning My Trade
>
> Your Umble Servant Henry Thomas Pardoe

Part of a leaf from a farmer's notebook, 1874:

April 29	Sowed Lettuce & planted Onions
May 1st	Planted Peas, sowed Onions & Tomatoes
13	Planted Potatoes, sowed Cabbage, egg plant & celery
14	Planted corn
15	Planted more peas
21	Sowed Lettuce pepper grass in the garden & picked Lettuce
29	Sowed more Cabbage, Lettuce and Celery in the hot bed
June 2nd, 3rd & 4th	Planted melons & Cucumbers & sowed flower seeds
8	Emma left for Saratoga
11	Set out Cabbage
14	Frost in many places none here

In these creased and dog-eared documents, in their phraseology, their spelling and their manifest sincerity, there is unique appeal. Products of the immediate moment, they were penned straight from the heart, without thought of more than the briefest survival. That so many of them remain is a minor miracle.

A note from a signwriter to his client, 1875:

> Sir Will you Pleas to Send And Let Mee Know What i am to Wright on the Wagon By return of Post it Would of Bin Writen to Day if i had of know Wot to Put on it
>
> Jacob Pike

A letter from a midshipman, off the coast of Guinea, 1793:

> Dear Uncle & Anty
> This Day we have taken a very rich prize to the amount of about £50000 of a French vesel homeward bound From the Eeas Indies Loaded with Indigo Sugar & Cotton, we was the first Ship that boarded, but there are seven othe India Ships that shares the same with us on that account there will be but little fore each mans Share but I hope we will have a good many more such like before we return — we are to send the prize to England & have taken the opertownity of informing you the pariculars I am very well preasant thank God for hoping this will find you the same give my best respectes to the D^r & Mrs Livingston, I hope you did receive the guinea I sent you to the care of Mr Tower we are now in the Latitude of 8 South and Longitude 22 aboute 25 Degrees from the Lands end I hope you will take care of my Sister till I return—I shall write you the first opertownity I mus conclude as the prize is now going to set sail from us—we have taken all the Frenchmen on board our Ship whill make a Large ships Company in all I like the busness very well, so I conclude & remayn
>
> your affectionate Nephew
> George Middleton

From Maidstone Prison, December 20, 1861:

> Sir,
> I should feel obliged by your seeing me today as I am anxious to know how I can proceed in procuring my discharge, and wish to explain my case to you.
>
> I am, Sir, You obed^t Servt
> Richard Thos. Lindsay

In a bill for six months' cleaning, washing and general work in the Church of St. Georges in the East, London, 1801, Sarah Granger (herself illiterate) enlists the help of a none-too-confident scribe:

To Mr Hutchinson the Head Church Warden of St Georges midelsex from the 25 of July to the 25 of January 1801——

	L	S	D
in Detter to Sarey Granger for Washen of 15 Surples for Church & Churchyard	1	17	6
the Comoun Cloth Napkin & take out the Stanes		0	10
Washen of 12 towels	0	0	6
Repairen the Surplies	0	2	0
the Bread for the westrey 7 times	0	3	6
Biscit for the westrey	0	2	2
Chipes for Liten the fires	0	7	0
Swipen 3 Chimbles in westrey	0	5	0
Gill Glas wite Stone bson & tin pot	0	1	5
turpintine for the Candell Diper	0	0	4
oile for the Lockes	0	0	2
Stone to Rub the Harth Scorunpaper		0	8
paper for the Sakerment Bread		0	2
the Comoun plate Chamber pot & Silv 3 times		2	0
Lemon to take the Stanes out of Surples		0	6
for Litten the fires Clening the westrey & Comoun		15	0
Lift on a mistake 7 threepney in the last but one for Bread		1	9
	4	0	6

Sett[d] this Bil the 20th July 1801

                              S Hutchinson
The Mark of   +   Sarah Granger

The eye may make a little heavy going, but the attentive ear may almost hear the very voice of yesterday.

The collector of handwritten ephemera enjoys a notable advantage: as a general rule, people are too busy to stop and decipher handwriting. As miscellanies are sorted over and the obvious items pick themselves out, the handwritten scraps tend to escape. And even the serious manuscript specialists—the Keats, Nelson and Lincoln hunters—they too, though literate, may ignore the apprentices and Sarey Grangers. As with the world of the printed page, to the ephemerist, it is the fallout that matters.

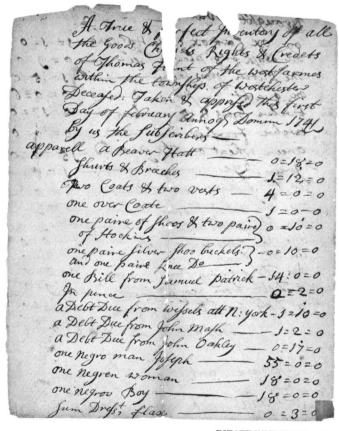

ESTATE INVENTORY, 1741

7

Finders, *Keepers*

When the embryonic ephemera collection begins to burst out of its first home in desk drawer or shoebox, the ephemerist comes to think seriously about the problem of filing, storage, display, and conservation. It also becomes clear that these matters are closely interlinked. No single aspect of the problem can be solved, it seems, without complicating the other.

It must be said immediately that up to now no one has satisfactorily solved any of these problems—let alone the problem as a whole. All that can be given here is a pointer or two to the way things appear to be moving; the rest is for personal exploration.

First, the problem of conservation. It has been truly said that among all the destructive agencies that beset ephemera—dust, dirt, acidification, heat, light, embrittlement and the rest—the most serious is the custodian himself. Whatever the field, magazines to trade cards, labels to leaflets, each time the material is handled it deteriorates. The process may be insidiously slow or horrifyingly fast, but the trend is always the same. First need is a means whereby, while remaining visible and accessible, the material is protected from ourselves.

For many classes of ephemera the obvious answer is the album—preferably with transparent sleeves or slots to protect specimens from handling and from chafing against each other. For multi-size collections, where specimens may include anything from half a ticket to a large poster, individual transparent envelopes may be the only (inadequate) answer. Whichever method is used, specimens should not be completely sealed in, trapping moisture and possible mold. For this reason, too, paper-backed display sleeves are preferable to the all-plastic variety. Porosity of the paper prevents specimens' becoming hermetically sealed.

Where items are mounted, two major precautions must be observed. Mounting paper (or board) must be acid-free, and adhesives must be water-soluble—preferably ordinary flour paste.

SMOKER'S SURPRISE:
NOVELTY
TRADE CARD, C. 1885

Acidity, of mounts or of specimens, is a serious hazard and may lead to embrittlement and eventual disintegration. It can be diagnosed by a litmus-paper test on a drop of distilled water placed on the surface to be tested. If the litmus paper turns red, acid is present. Deacidification may be carried out by dusting items with calcium carbonate powder or by enclosing sachets of the powder in specimen boxes, drawers, or other containers.

Flour paste is the preferred mountant, not only because it is water-soluble, and allows the specimen to be soaked off its mount without damage, but because it is harmless to surfaces. In almost every other form of adhesive there is chemical migration between paper, adhesive and mount, resulting in stains or other damage.

Gummed photo-corners may be used for small items. So may stamp hinges—though these also may not be entirely above suspicion. Contact adhesive tapes of any kind, handiest of all fixing gadgets, are also the most disastrous. They shrink, wrinkle, ooze and discolor. They also irremediably stain the surface they adhere to. Most catastrophic of all, they tear surfaces on removal. (Old tape "repairs" may be treated by gently brushing with carbon tetrachoride—though the fumes of this are best avoided if the collector is to continue to enjoy his ephemera. The liquid dissolves the adhesive, allowing the tape to be gently peeled away. But the stain remains forever. No one has yet devised an antidote.)

Professional repairs are done with flour paste and repair paper or repair silk, both available from specialist suppliers. Repair paper is used as a backing for single-sided documents. Where printing or writing is present on both sides, silk is used. The material is so fine as to be more or less invisible and impairs legibility only very slightly. It should be stressed however that repair work is a job for experts. The rank-and-file ephemerist aspires only to the simpler operations. Clearly, it is only in the more precious of ancient items that delicate repair work will be needed. For the most part the collector will seek to carry out only the first part of the professional repairer's work: "to arrest decay and protect from further damage."

Most items may be cleaned by rubbing lightly with an art eraser. This comes in a solid block or granulated as a powder. Items may also be laid on a suitable surface and gently moistened with tap water, the face of the specimen being lightly dabbed with a moist sponge. (Rubbing with the sponge is to be avoided; all that is needed is a gentle dabbing movement.) Before moistening the item to be cleaned it should be checked for color fastness. A corner of blotting paper dipped in a single drop of water or the surface to be checked will indicate whether or not inks, colors or writing will run when wet. If the blotting paper picks up any trace, dry cleaning is indicated.

Some collectors extend the cleaning process by bleaching. This produces an effect of quite startling whiteness—some would say an unnatural pallor. The process also has the effect of removing all but the faintest trace of ink handwriting; it should be used only with care. After a preliminary bath in clean water, the document is flooded in a weak solution of ordinary domestic bleaching fluid. Printing will remain; all else will fade. The item is thoroughly washed in running water for twenty to thirty minutes, sized to restore its crispness, and dried under light pressure between sheets of blotting paper. Sizing is simply a matter of immersing the item in a weak solution (one teaspoonful to half a pint of water) of good quality decorator's size.

It must be said that, on the whole, the less treatment an item receives the better. As with operations on ourselves, therapy may be a shock to the system. And so far as the cosmetic aspect of cleaning and repair is concerned, most collectors prefer their exhibits to look their age. There is something deeply disturbing—*suspect* even—about an 18th-Century proclamation that looks as though it had been printed yesterday. Crumples and creases, honorable battle scars of real life, are part of the deal.

A word about the filing of ephemera. This also is something no one has yet fully sorted out. Certainly if a collection is to be more than a mere accumulation, there must be some way of finding individual items quickly. Collections grow surprisingly fast; while initially the collector knows what he has and where it all is, the stage soon comes when he can no longer keep pace with his collection. A card index, a loose-leaf catalog—something, sooner or later, must come to the rescue.

Filing, display, storage, and conservation are, as we have seen, interlocking problems. Whatever organizing methods are finally adopted, the collector does well to fix on a good one before too long. It is also as well to be sure methods meet the long-term need. A change of organization in mid-stream, involving the re-siting and re-indexing of possibly thousands of items, is no fun at all. Nor is a too-long-delayed attempt to save the day, when the overburden of unsorted material has become unmanageable.

To the new ephemerist, such solemn thoughts may seem premature. But it is always a little later than we think.

1893 FANTAIL

Books and Useful Addresses

Following are a few publications, institutions, dealers, and societies of interest to the ephemerist.

BOOKS

Collecting Printed Ephemera, John Lewis, London, 1976.

Discovering Theatre Ephemera, John Kennedy Melling, Aylesbury, 1974.

Label Design: the evolution, design and function of labels from the earliest times to the present day, Claude Humbert, London, 1972.

Packaging and Print, Alec Davis, London, 1967.

Printed Ephemera: the changing use of type and letterforms in English and American Printing, John Lewis, London and New York, 1962. The definitive work by Mr. Lewis; any collector who can locate a copy should consider himself fortunate indeed.

Printing 1770-1970, Michael Twyman, London, 1970.

The Public Notice: an Illustrative History, Maurice Rickards, Newton Abbot, 1973.

Victorian Delights, Robert Wood, London and New York, 1967.

PERIODICALS

United States

Antique Trader Weekly, P.O. Box 1050, Dubuque, Iowa 52001

Bookman's Weekly, P.O. Box AB, Clifton, NJ 47015

Graphic Americana, 62 Hampshire Street, Portland, ME 04011

Masthead (newspaper collecting), P.O. Box 1009, Marblehead, MA 01945

Great Britain

Antique News, 29 Parkfield Road, Stourbridge, W. Midlands DY8 1HD

The Ephemerist, 10 Fitzroy Square, London WIP 5AH

Postcard Collectors Gazette, 3 Chester Gate, London NWI

DEALERS

United States

Americana Mail Auction, 4015 Kilmer Avenue, Allentown, PA 18105

Ann Phillips Antiques, 899 Madison Avenue, New York, NY 10021

Antiques Americana, Box 19, N. Abington, MA 02351
Goodspeed's Book Shop, 18 Beacon Street, Boston, MA 02108
Harris Auction Galleries, 873 N. Howard Street, Baltimore, MD 21201
Miscellaneous Man, Box 1776, New Freedom, PA 17349
Samuel Murray, Wilbraham, MA 01950

Europe

Henry Bristow, 105 Southampton Road, Ringwood, Hants, England
Le Grenier du Collectionneur, 238 avenue Orban, Brussels, Belgium
Desiderata, Postfach 5362, D-78 Freiburg, West Germany
Ian Hodgkins, 37 Connaught Street, London W2, England
Ken Lawson, 24 Watford Road, Wembley, Middlesex HAO 3EP, England
Pleasures of Past Times, 11 Cecil Court, London WC2, England
Sebastian d'Orsai, 6 Kensington Mall, London W8, England
Brian Swallow, 2 Beaufort West, London Road, Bath BA1 6QB, England

MUSEUMS, LIBRARIES, COLLECTIONS

United States

American Antiquarian Society, Worcester, Massachusetts
Historical Society of Pennsylvania, Philadelphia
Houghton Library, Cambridge, Massachusetts
Library of Congress, Washington, D.C.
New-York Historical Society, New York
New York Public Library, New York

Great Britain

British Museum, London
British Railway Museum, York
Guildhall Library, London
John Johnson Collection, Bodleian Library, Oxford
Museum of British Rural Life, Reading
Museum of London
Pepysian Library, Cambridge
Science Museum, London
St. Bride Printing Library, London
Victoria and Albert Museum, London

Index

BUSINESS CARD, C. 1977